Dedicated To
All The Learners
Beginning Their
Journey

ISBN-13: 979-8-878277-13-6

This Workbook Belongs To

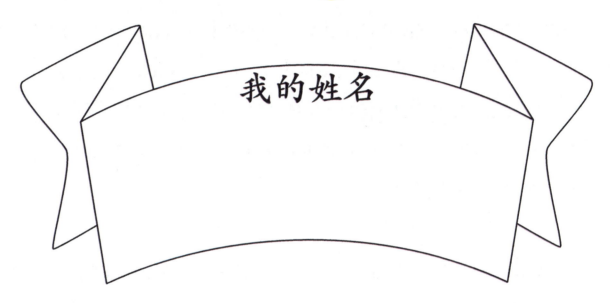

我的姓名

Hello! 你好!

Welcome to Traditional Chinese For Kids Made Easy Book 2. This book is intended to provide a fun, simple, and easy way for you to learn traditional Chinese. These characters will start your journey towards Chinese mastery!

You will find 50 illustrative pages with Pinyin, English, color-in pictures, and character strokes to follow in red. Don't worry too much about the stroke width.

Grab a pen or pencil and follow along. Let's start your journey! 加油!

Contents

yī

一

One

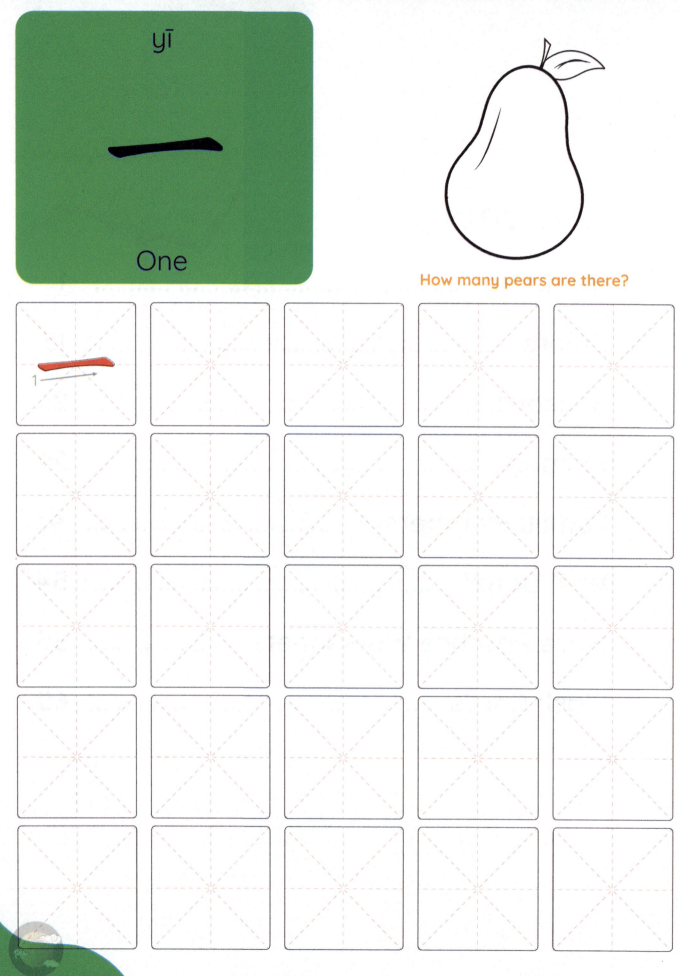

How many pears are there?

1

1

How many cherries are together?

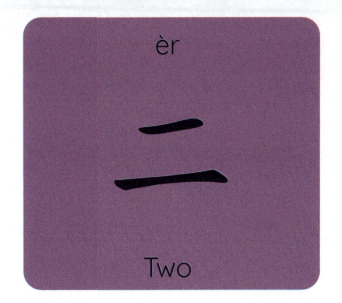

èr

二

Two

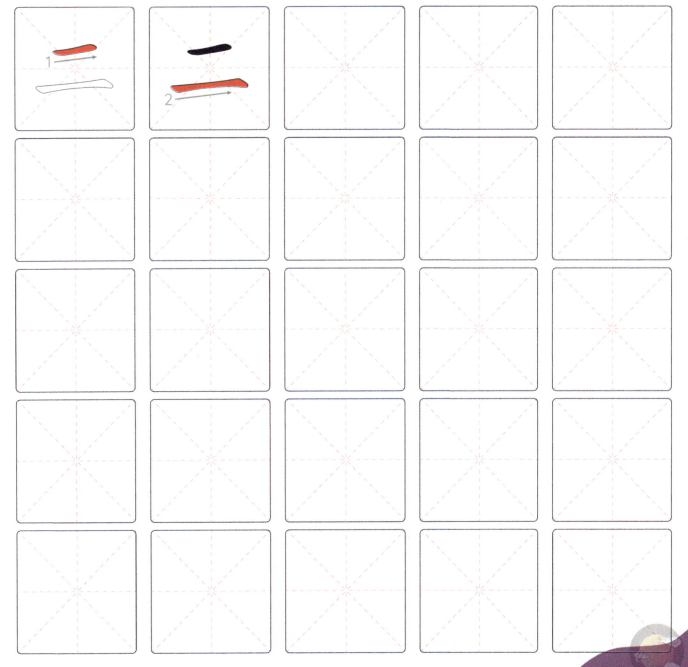

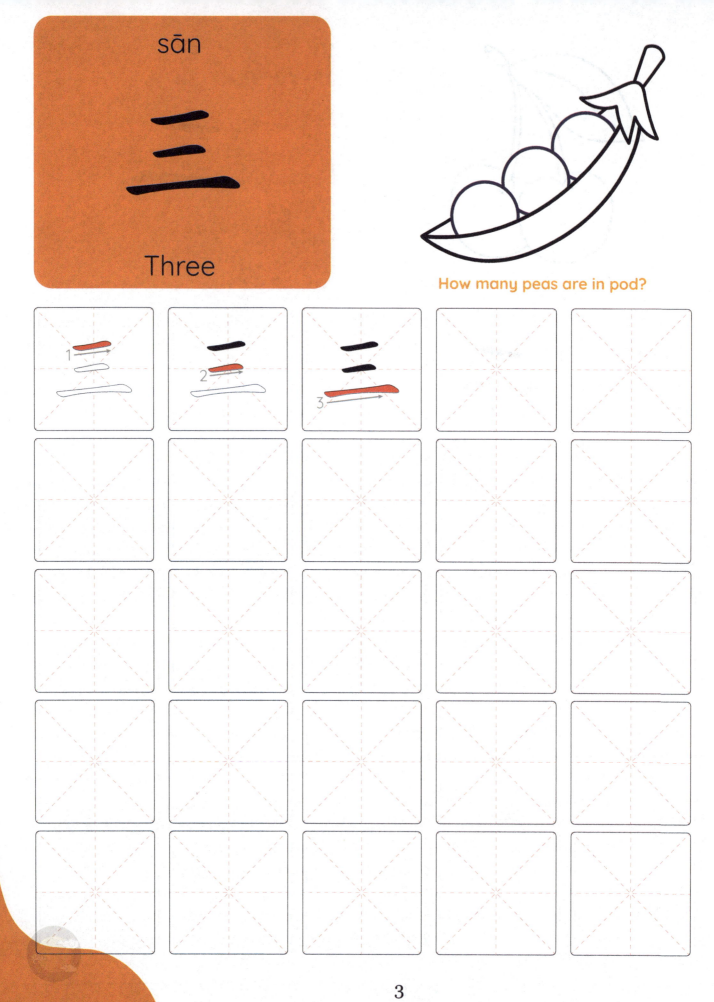

sān

Three

How many peas are in pod?

Four

How many corns are together?

wǔ

五

Five

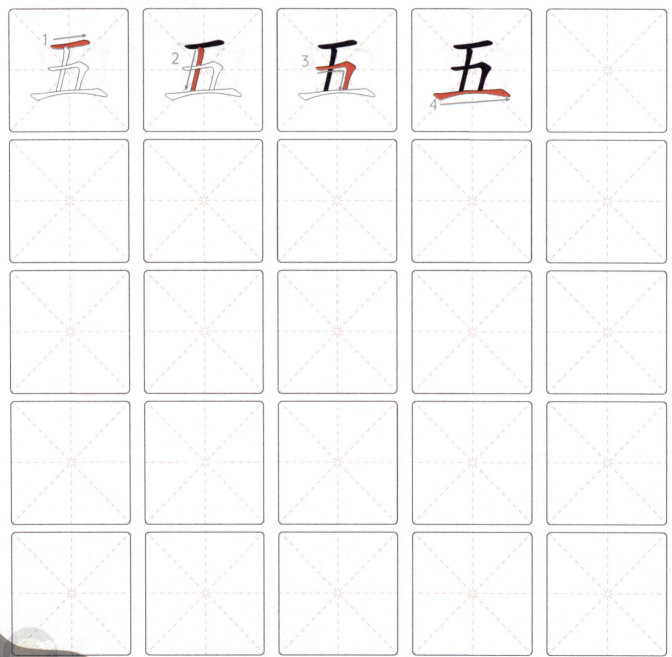

liù

六

Six

Count the number of flower petals.

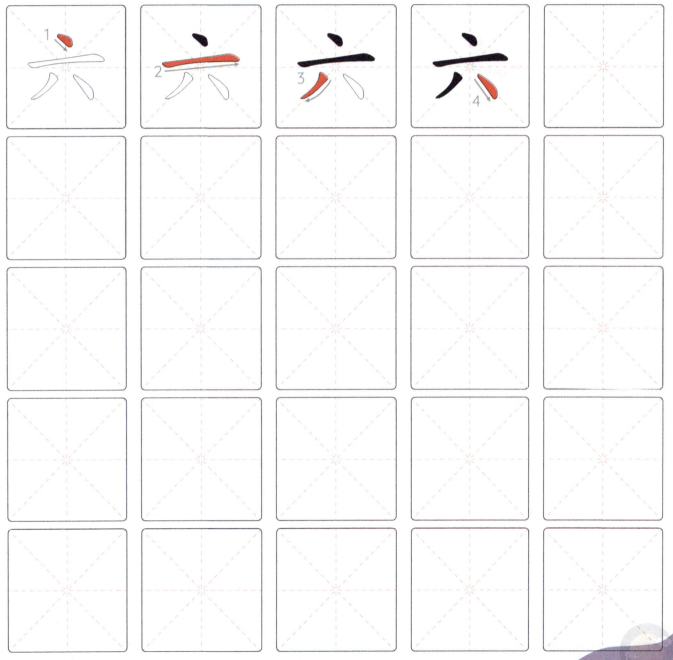

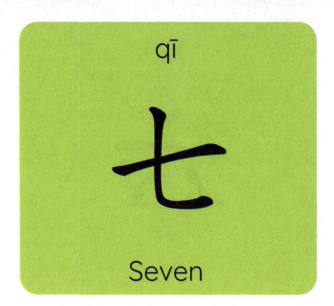

qī

Seven

Count the number of house keys.

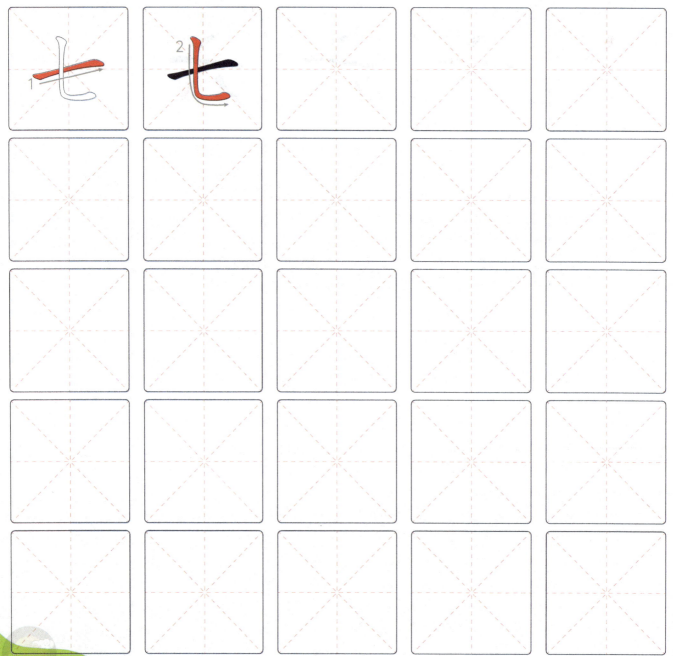

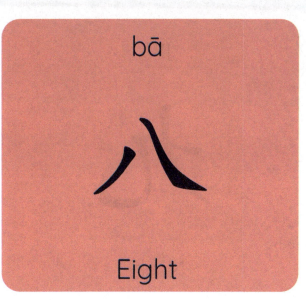

bā

八

Eight

How many apples are there?

jiǔ

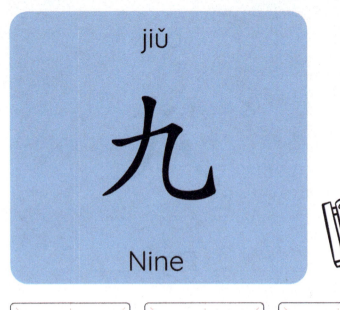

Nine

Count the number of toys!

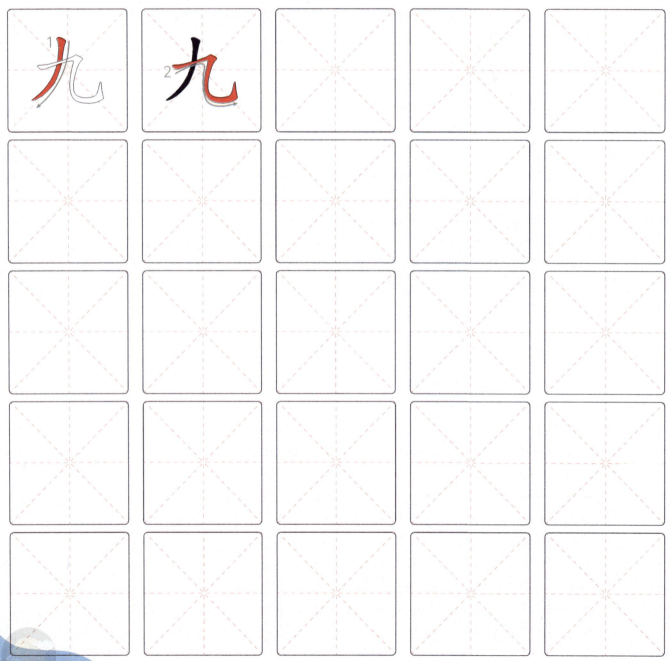

9

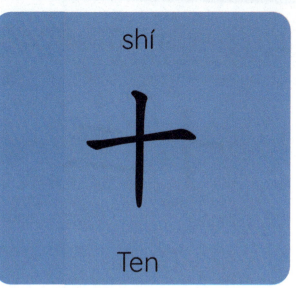

shí

Ten

How many fingers are there?

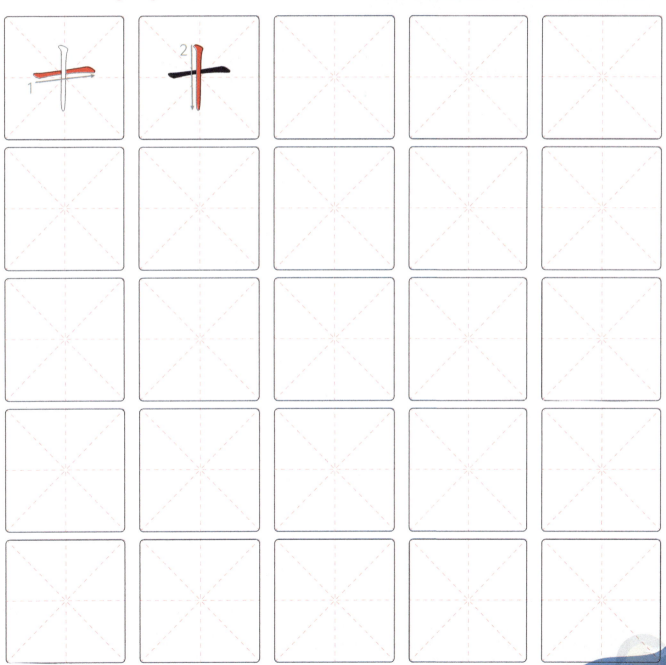

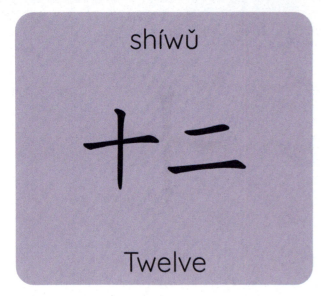

shíwǔ

十二

Twelve

How many eggs are in the boxes?

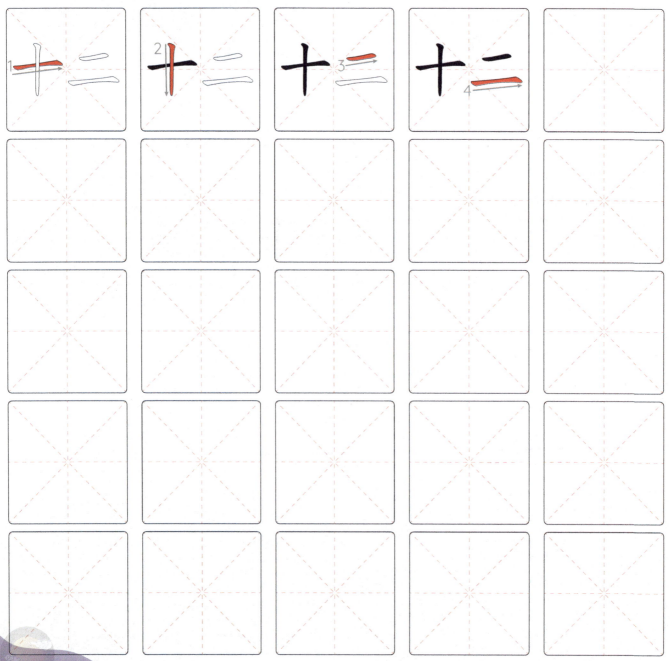

Wohoo! You counted all the way to 20!

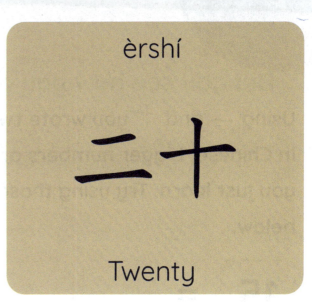

èrshí

二十

Twenty

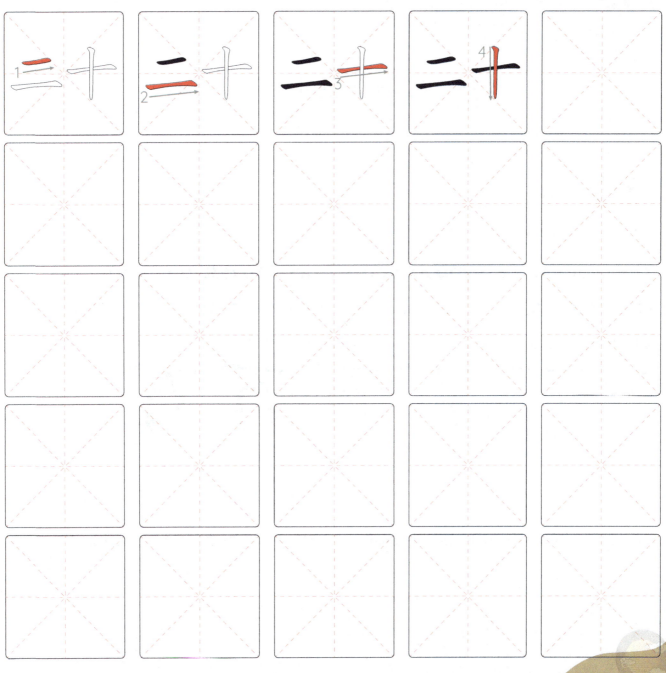

Did you see how you did twelve and twenty?

Using 二 and 十 you wrote twelve and twenty.

In Chinese, bigger numbers are written using the some charcters you just learn. Try using those characters and writing the numbers below.

15 = ☐ ☐

十 七 = ☐

30 = ☐ ☐

There are some numbers you will need to add an extra character to count bigger numbers. Lets learn to write 100!

We will need 一 and 百. 百 = hundred (bǎi)

To write one hundred, we put 一 and 百 together to make yībǎi.

Lets draw a line from the number to its character!

sè

色

Color

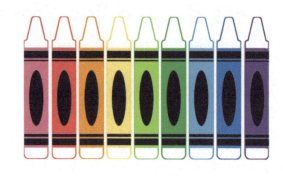

How many colors do you see? The rest of the pictures are for you to color in!

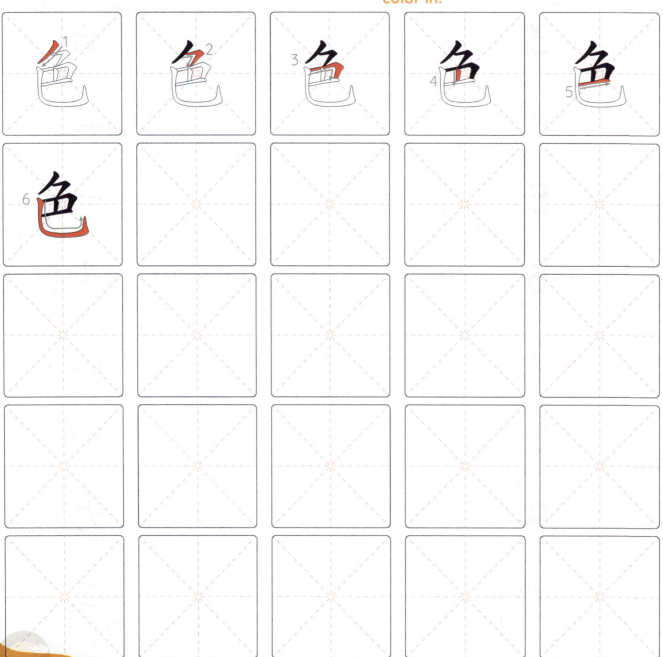

紅

Red

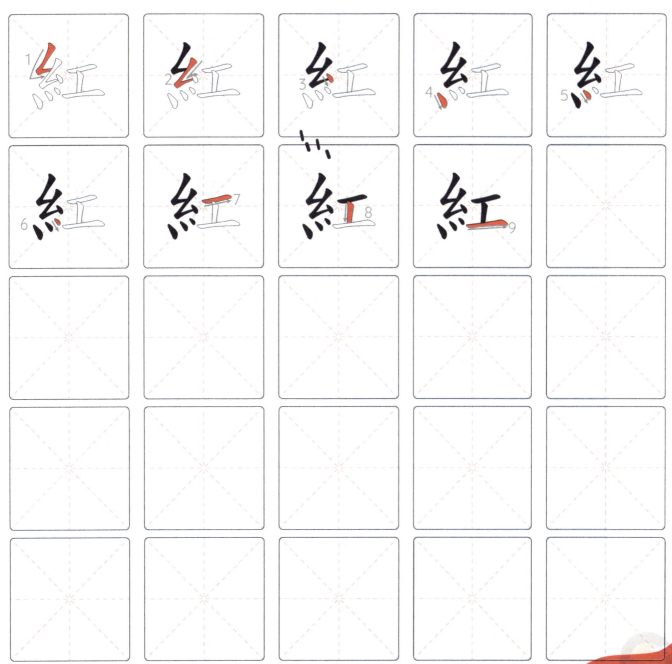

huáng

黄

Yellow

  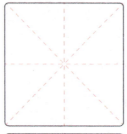 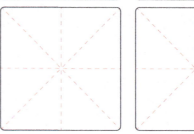

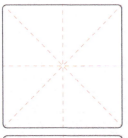 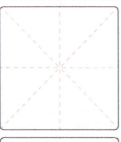  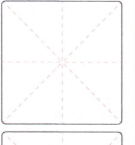 

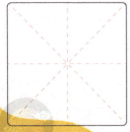 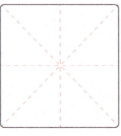 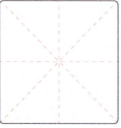 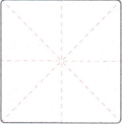

lǜ

綠

Green

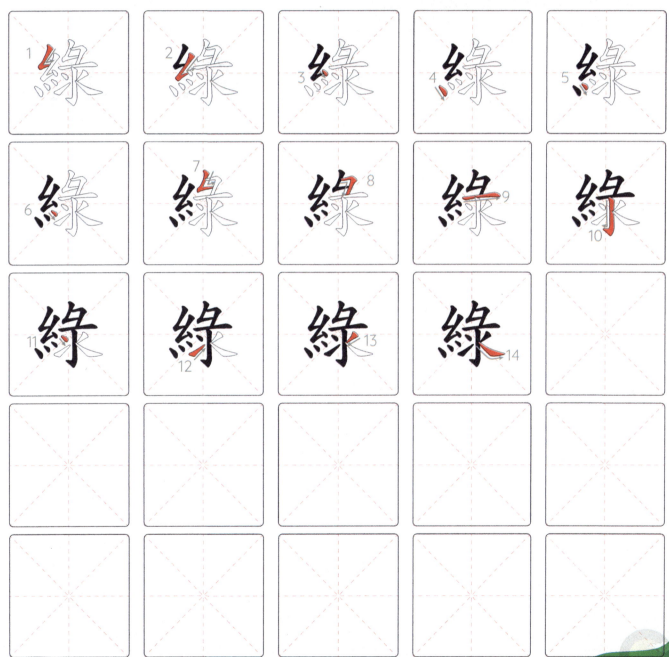

bái

白

White

黑

Black

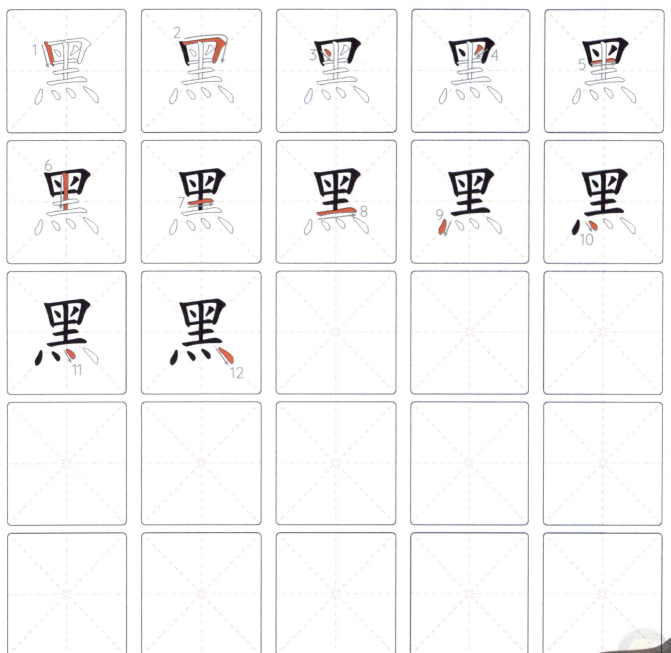

zōng

棕

Brown

紫

Purple

chūn

春

Spring

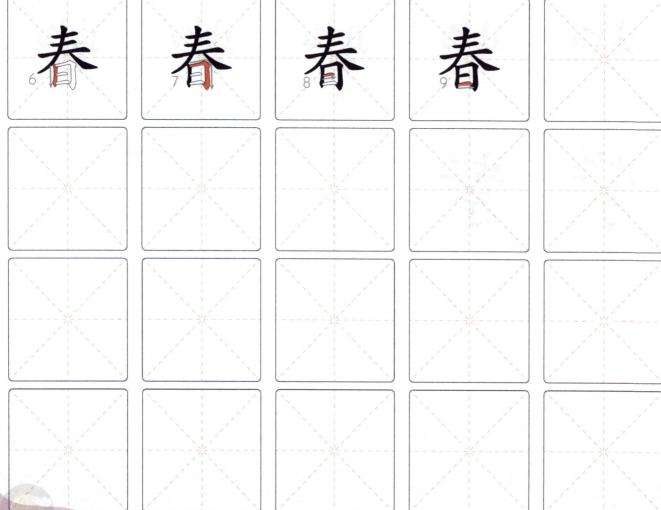

xià

夏

Summer

qiū

秋

Fall

25

Let's Match The Season!

Match the below season characters with the different pictures.

hóu

猴

Monkey

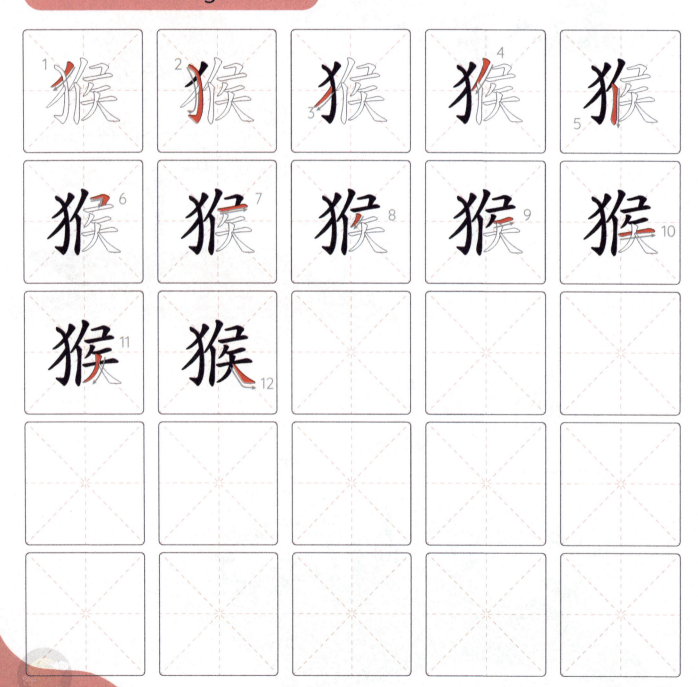

虎

Tiger

tù

兔

Rabbit

yú

魚

Fish

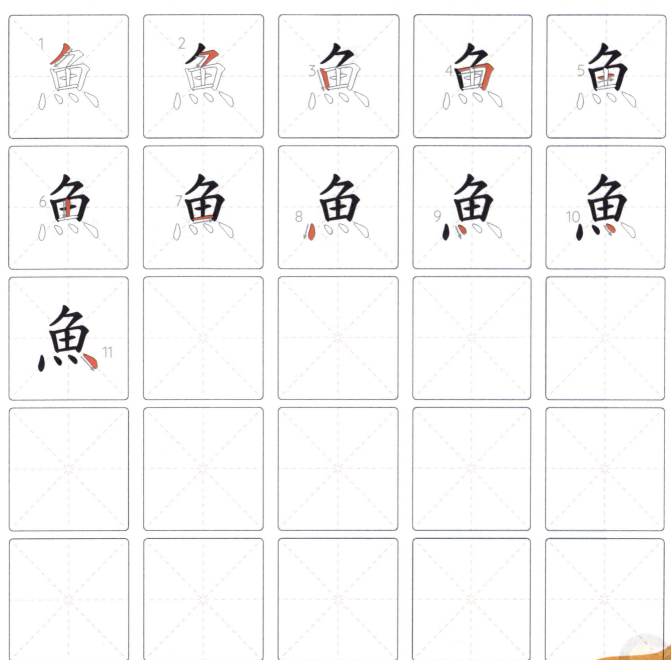

mǎ

馬

Horse

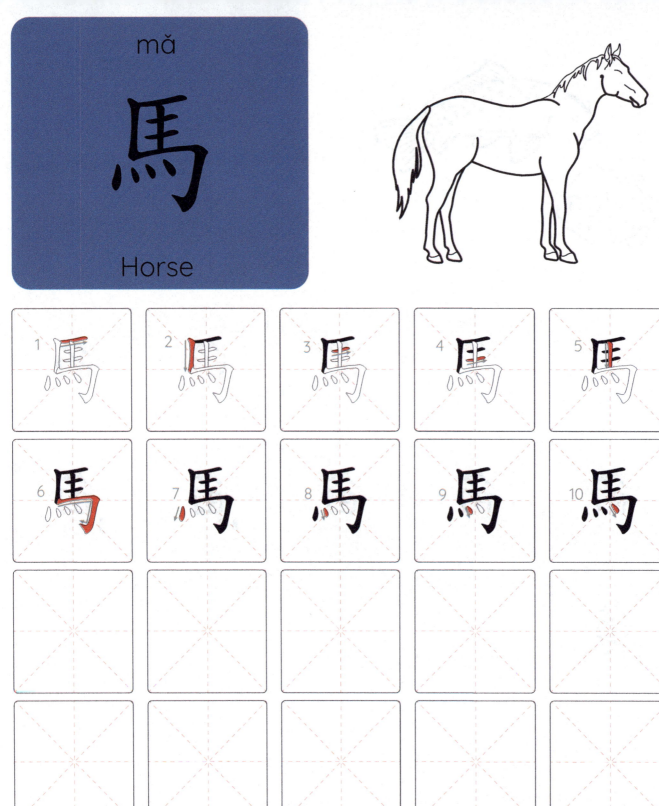

yáng

羊

Sheep

niú

牛

Cow

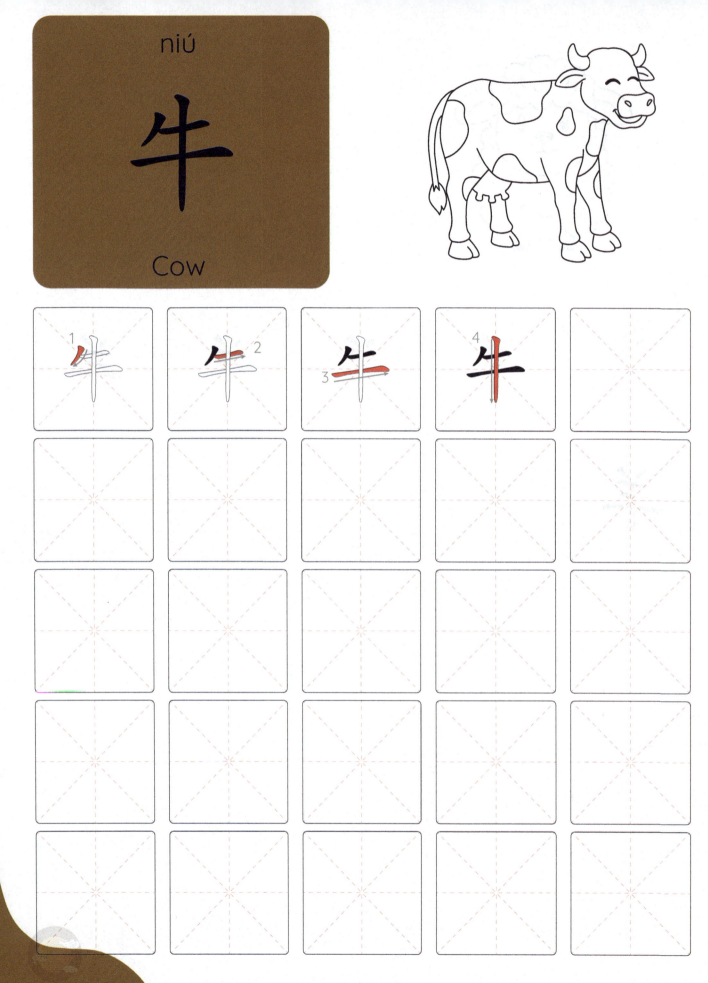

chóng

蟲

Insect

niǎo

鳥

Bird

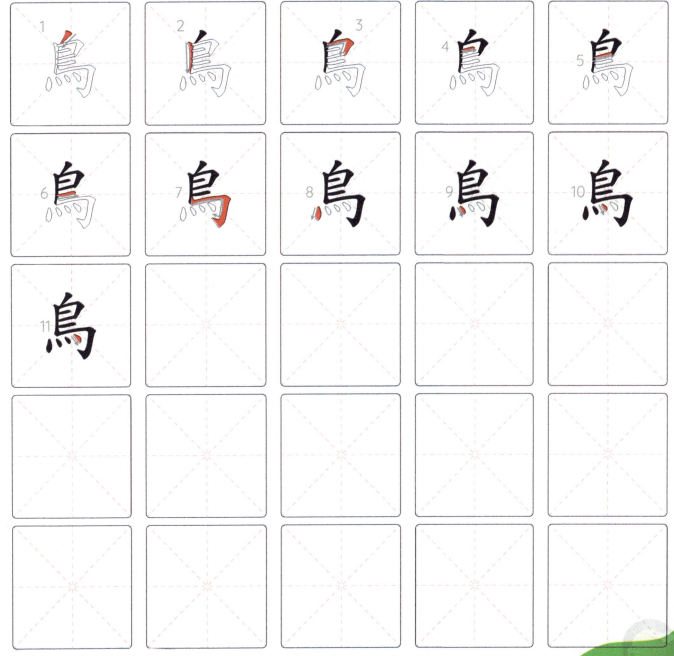

38

hú

狐

Fox

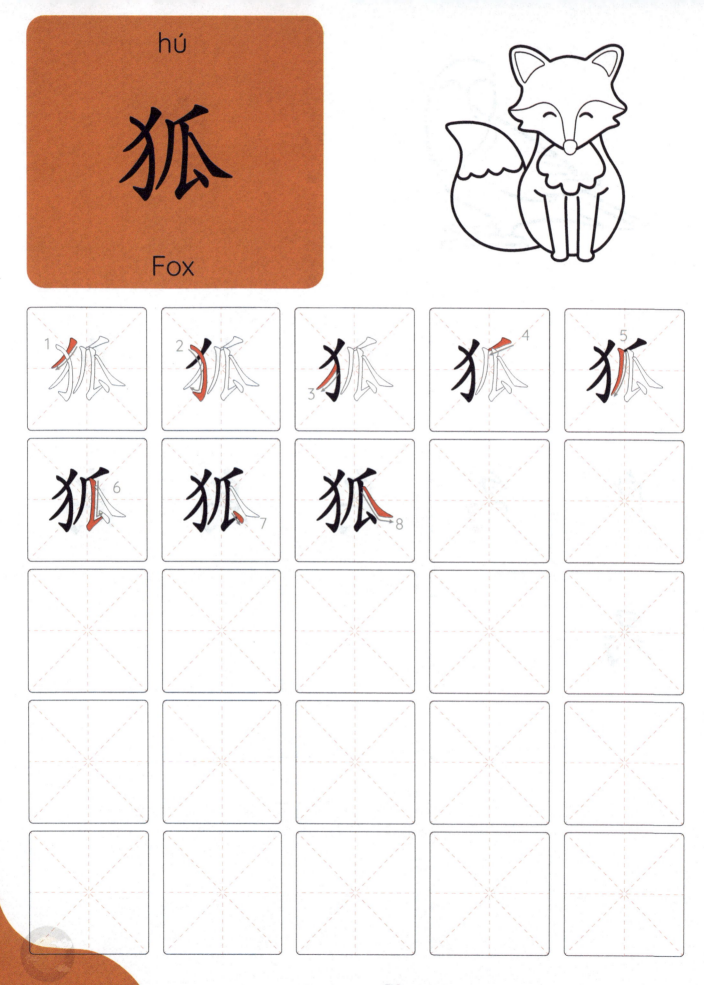

象

Elephant

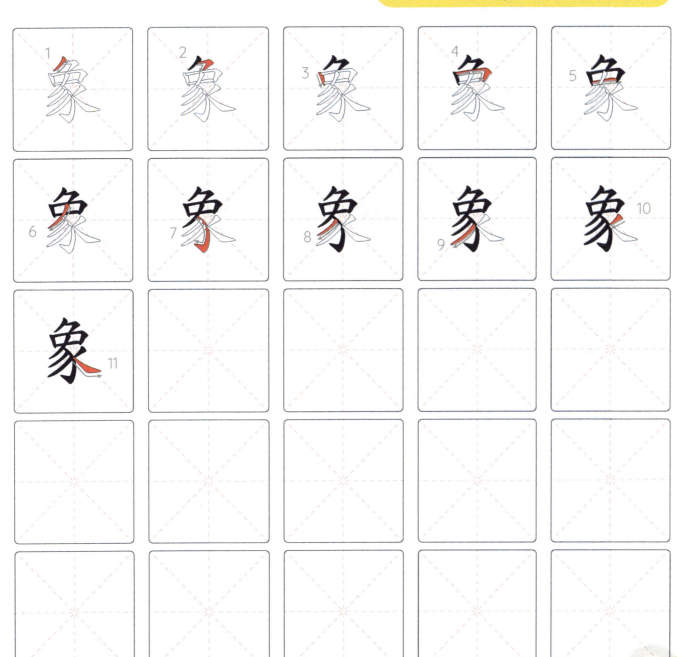

shé

蛇

Snake

   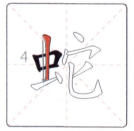 

熊

Bear

jiā

家

Family

māmā

媽媽

Mom

    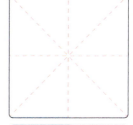

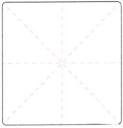 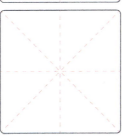 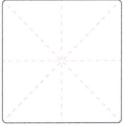 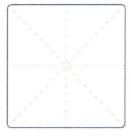 

bàba

爸爸

Dad

jiě jie

姐姐

Older Sister

gēgē

哥哥

Older Brother

妹妹

Younger Sister

dìdì

弟弟

Younger Brother

49

nǎinai

奶奶

Grandma

yéyé

爺爺

Grandpa

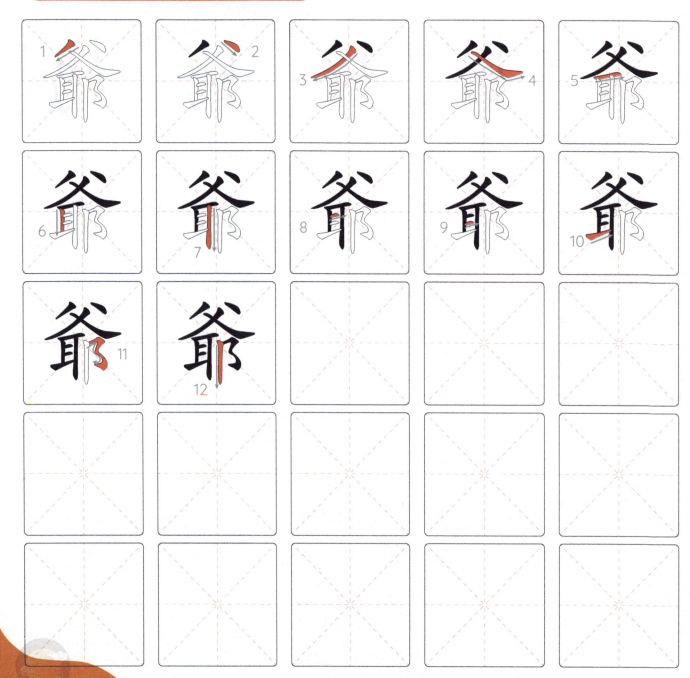

yíyí

阿姨

Aunt

  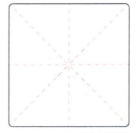 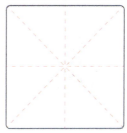 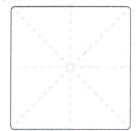

    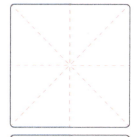

  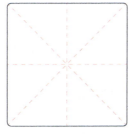 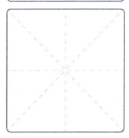 

shūshu

叔叔

Uncle

Well Done!

You mastered all these characters!

一 二 三 四 五 六 七 八 九 十

十 二 百 色 紅 黃 綠 白 黑 棕
二 十

紫 春 夏 秋 冬 猴 虎 兔 魚 馬

羊 牛 狗 蟲 鳥 狐 象 蛇 熊 家

媽 爸 姐 哥 妹 弟 奶 爺 姨 叔

More Practice!

Use the squares to practice the characters you just learned.

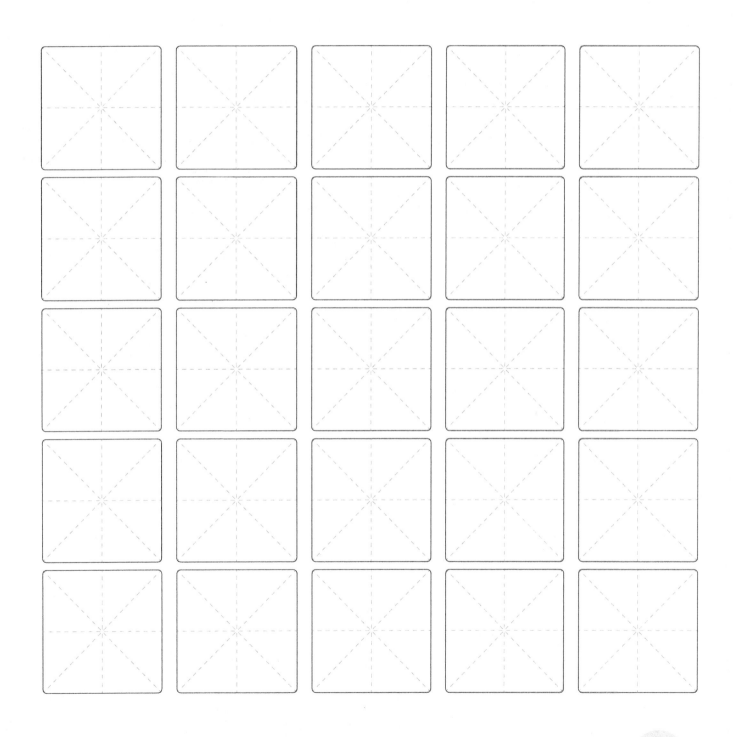

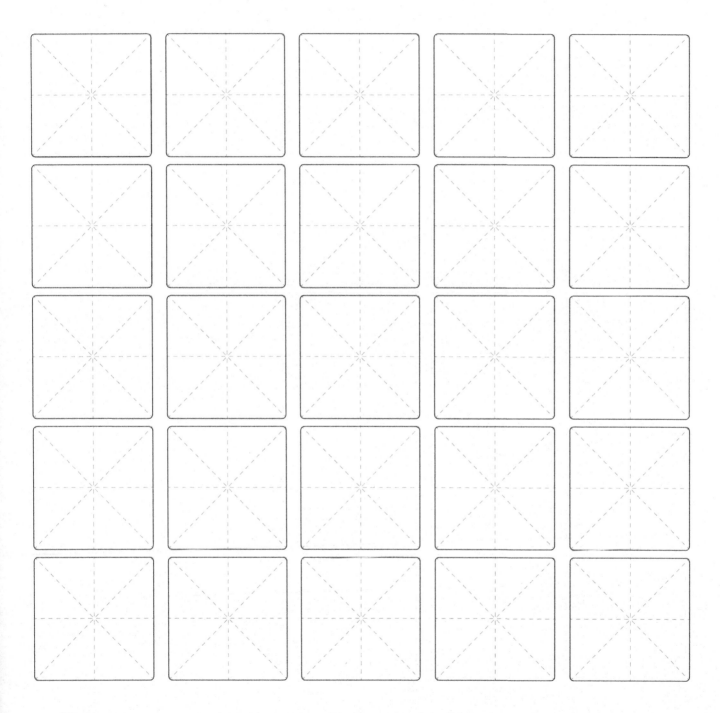

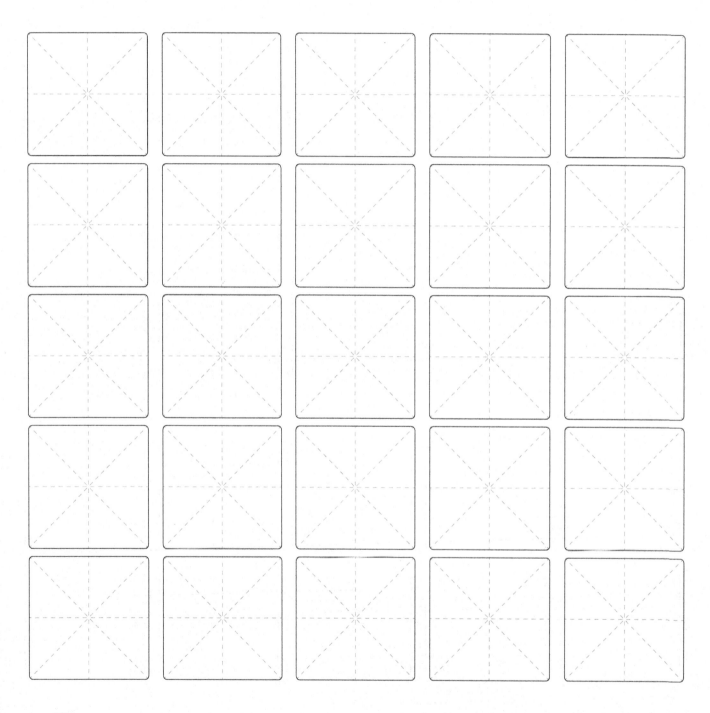

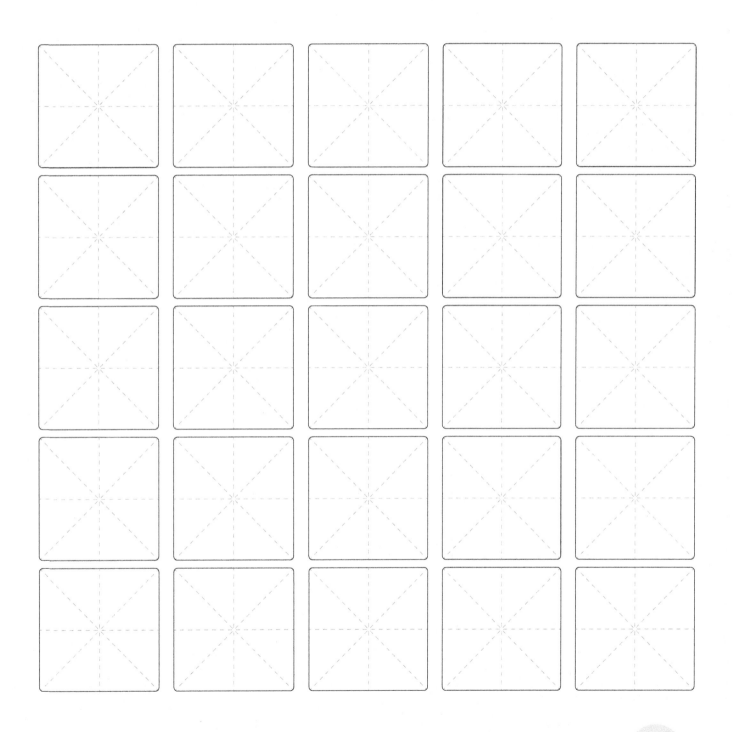

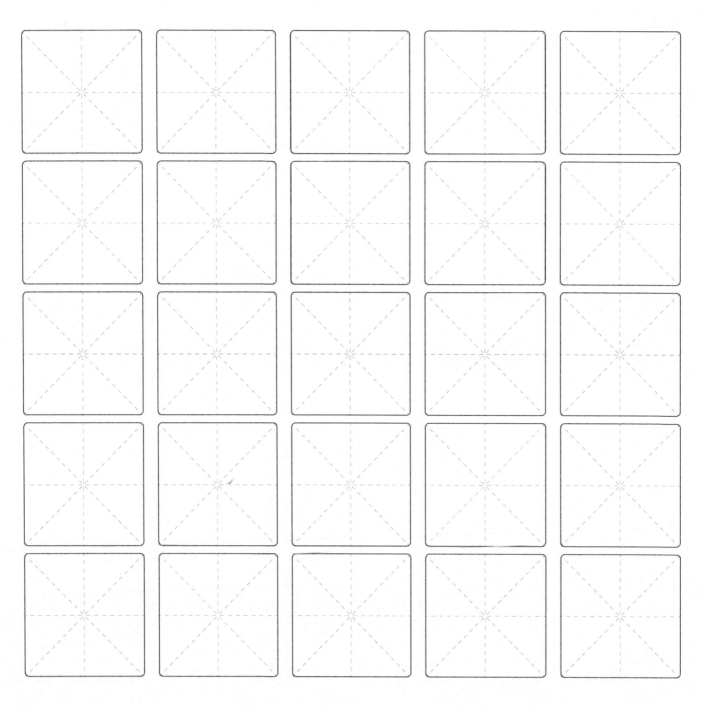

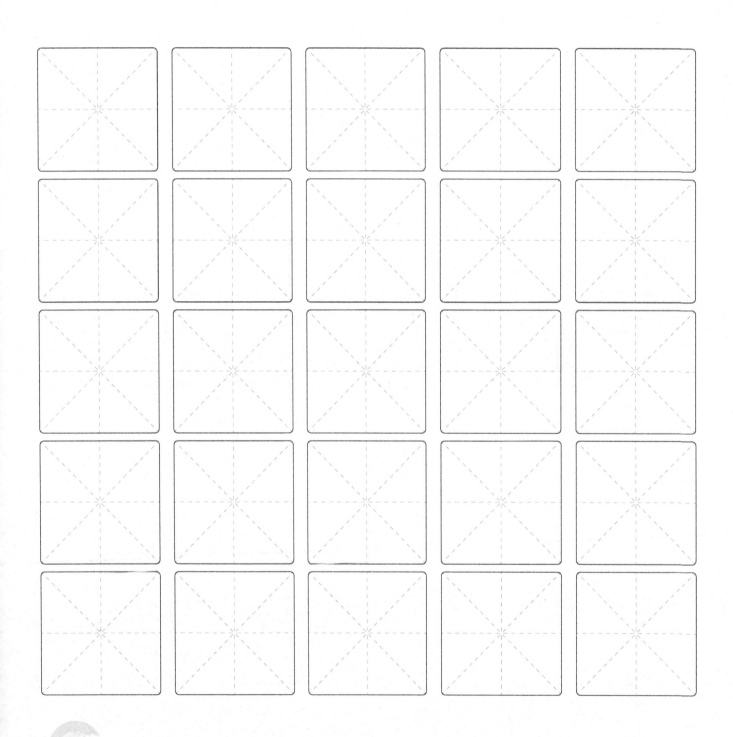

Intentionally Left Blank

yī

一

One

èr

二

Two

sān

三

Three

sì

四

Four

wǔ

五

Five

liù

六

Six

Two Cherries

One Pear

Four Corn

Three Peas in the Pod

Six Flower Petals

Five Point Star

qī

七

Seven

bā

八

Eight

jiǔ

九

Nine

shí

十

Ten

shíwǔ

十二

Twelve

èrshí

二十

Twenty

Eight Apples

Seven House Keys

Ten Fingers

Nine Toys

Twenty

Twelve Eggs

bǎi

百

Hundred

sè

色

Color

hóngsè

紅

Red

huángsè

黃

Yellow

lǜ sè

綠

Green

báisè

白

White

Colors

One Hundred

Yellow

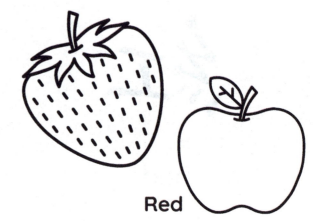

Red

White

Green

hēi	zōng
黑	棕
Black	Brown

zǐ	chūn
紫	春
Purple	Spring

xià	qiū
夏	秋
Summer	Fall

Brown

Black

Spring

Purple

Fall

Summer

dōng

冬

Winter

hóu

猴

Monkey

hǔ

虎

Tiger

tù

兔

Rabbit

yú

魚

Fish

mǎ

馬

Horse

Monkey

Winter

Rabbit

Tiger

Horse

Fish

yáng

羊

Sheep

niú

牛

Cow

gǒu

狗

Dog

chóng

蟲

Insect

niǎo

鳥

Bird

hú

狐

Fox

Cow

Sheep

Insect

Dog

Fox

Bird

xiàng

象

Elephant

shé

蛇

Snake

xióng

熊

Bear

jiā

家

Family

māmā

媽媽

Mom

bàba

爸爸

Dad

Snake

Elephant

Family

Bear

Dad

Mom

jiě jie	gēgē
姐姐	哥哥
Older Sister	Older Brother

mèimei	dìdì
妹妹	弟弟
Younger Sister	Younger Brother

nǎinai	yéyé
奶奶	爺爺
Grandma	Grandpa

Older Brother

Older Sister

Younger Brother

Younger Sister

Grandpa

Grandma

yíyí

阿姨

Aunt

shūshu

叔叔

Uncle

Uncle

Aunt

Thank You For
Supporting
Small Business

Check out
Sunset Learners Club's
other learning
material on Amazon

Made in the USA
Columbia, SC
08 March 2025

54865355R10050